Newbridge Discovery Links®

HURRICANES

Joseph K. Brennan

Newbridge
A Haights Cross Communications Company

Hurricanes
ISBN: 1-58273-727-4

Program Author: Dr. Brenda Parkes, Literacy Expert
Content Reviewer: Dr. Chris Landsea, National Oceanic and Atmospheric Administration (NOAA),
 Hurricane Research Division, Miami, FL
Teacher Reviewer: Sherri Strating, Horace Mann Lab School, Northwest Missouri State University,
 Maryville, MO

Written by Joseph K. Brennan

Newbridge Educational Publishing
333 East 38th Street, New York, NY 10016
www.newbridgeonline.com

Cover Photograph: Hurricane Gilbert hitting Jamaica in 1988
Table of Contents Photograph: Hurricane waves sweeping a beach

Photo Credits
Cover: The Purcell Team/CORBIS; Table of Contents page: Mark Richards/PhotoEdit/Picturequest;
pages 4–5: National Oceanic and Atmospheric Administration/Department Of Commerce, (inset)
Robin Hill/Index Stock; page 6: CORBIS; page 7: CORBIS; pages 8–9: Scott Dommin; pages 10–14:
National Oceanic and Atmospheric Administration/Department of Commerce; page 15: AFP/CORBIS;
page 16: Tyler Hicks/*Wilmington Star News*; page 17: Warren Faidley/Weatherstock; page 18: Mike
Brown/Liaison; page 19: Hotstock/Stock Connection/Picturequest; pages 20–21: Mark Richards/
PhotoEdit/Picturequest; page 22: Dave Martin/APA; pages 24–25: J. Christopher/Weatherstock;
page 26: Reuters NewMedia, Inc./CORBIS; page 27: Raymond Gehman/CORBIS, (inset) Tony
Arruza/CORBIS; page 28: Chuck Carlton/Index Stock; page 29: Gallo Images/CORBIS; page 30:
Kyle Krause/Index Stock

Illustrations on pages 14 and 23 by Ivy Rutzky

10 9 8 7 6 5 4 3

Table of Contents

Flying into the Heart of the Storm

Torrents of rain lash the plane as it flies through the tropical storm. Lightning flashes in every direction. Sudden gusts of wind toss the plane about as if it were a matchstick. The six crew members are strapped into their seats with safety harnesses. All the scientific equipment is tied down.

The six crew members are **hurricane hunters**. Their mission is to fly back and forth through hurricanes and other tropical storms to collect vital information. Hurricane hunters are part of a weather prediction system that tracks storms as they develop and move across the Atlantic Ocean, Caribbean Sea, and Gulf of Mexico.

Each year, from June to November, hurricanes pose a threat to the millions of people who live along the Atlantic and Gulf Coasts of the United States.

The **tropical storm** that's buffeting the airplane with fierce wind and torrential rain started when an area of **low pressure** formed over warm ocean waters. Air began to rotate around this area of low pressure, and thunderstorms started to gather, forming a **tropical depression**. When the winds soared above 38 miles per hour (mph), it became a tropical storm, and the flying weather crew was sent to gather information about it.

This photograph taken from the space shuttle *Columbia* shows clouds spiraling around an area of low pressure.

A view of Hurricane Elena taken from space shows the immense size of a hurricane. A fully developed hurricane can stretch for hundreds of miles.

If the wind becomes stronger than 73 mph, the storm will be classified as a hurricane. And the hurricane hunters will continue to monitor the storm as it grows worse. If they do fly through a hurricane, their prop-driven plane will be subjected to the most destructive weather force on earth. The worst hurricanes have winds of some 150 mph to 190 mph. They generate as much energy as 200 times the world's entire electrical energy output for a single day.

The crew collects data on the force of the winds, the storm's position, and the air pressure, temperature, and humidity. All this data is transmitted to the National Hurricane Center in Miami, Florida.

The data the hurricane hunters gather from the storm's **eye** is particularly important. It provides the hurricane center with the most accurate measurement of the storm's intensity and location.

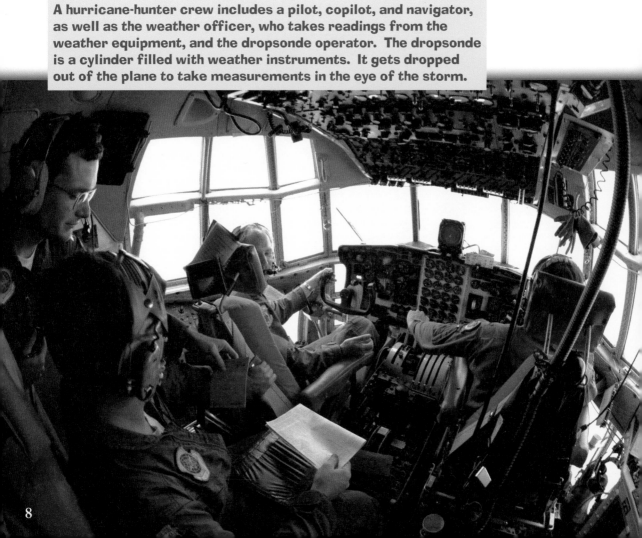

A hurricane-hunter crew includes a pilot, copilot, and navigator, as well as the weather officer, who takes readings from the weather equipment, and the dropsonde operator. The dropsonde is a cylinder filled with weather instruments. It gets dropped out of the plane to take measurements in the eye of the storm.

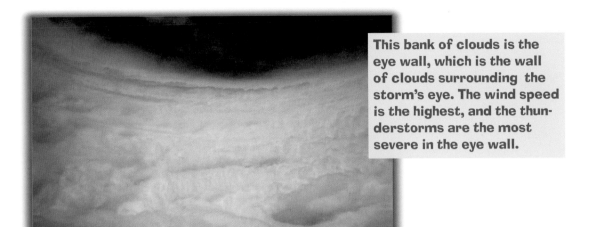

This bank of clouds is the eye wall, which is the wall of clouds surrounding the storm's eye. The wind speed is the highest, and the thunderstorms are the most severe in the eye wall.

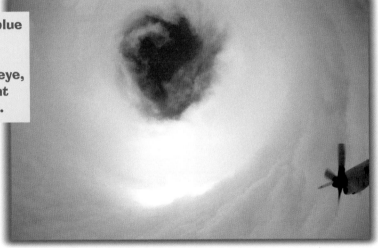

Sometimes a patch of blue sky appears above the plane as the hurricane hunters fly through the eye, which is the calm area at the center of the storm.

The plane flies at least 105 miles from the eye to the outer reaches of the tropical storm to map the extent of the damaging winds. Every two hours, the aircraft passes through the eye and the punishing **eye wall** that surrounds the eye. It will continue in this X pattern until the next plane is ready to take its place in the around-the-clock surveillance of the developing storm.

Tracking the Storm

The storm's wind is knocking about the hurricane hunters' plane and sending the crew straining against their safety harnesses. Rain falls so hard that the crew can't see the plane's wingtips. Measuring instruments indicate that the wind has reached 74 mph. The plane is now flying through a hurricane.

The hurricane is moving across the Atlantic Ocean, but it is still hundreds of miles from land. The storm may blow itself out. But it may also strike land. If the hurricane's path isn't predicted correctly, it can cause massive loss of life.

In the past, there was no way to predict where or when a hurricane would strike. Hurricanes could catch people totally by surprise.

The hurricane that hit Galveston, Texas, in 1900 was the worst natural disaster in U.S. history.

Before the 1938 hurricane hit, many people who lived along the New England coast didn't know a big storm was on its way. Then the wind started to howl.

In 1900, a hurricane struck Galveston, Texas. The city was unprepared, and no one had been evacuated from the houses and buildings that lined the coast. During the storm, a fifteen-foot **storm surge** swept over Galveston. One building after another crumbled as the wall of water moved through the city, leaving people helpless in the surging water. More than 6,000 Galveston residents died.

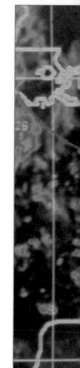

HURRICANE ANDREW
16 - 28 AUG 1992

    Today, while scientists can't stop hurricanes, they can warn
people of their approach. Hurricane hunters are only one of
the ways they can do this.

    Meteorologists begin tracking and studying hurricanes from
the time the tropical depression makes its first appearance. They
study the storm's progress with the help of **weather satellites** and
weather balloons.

    At the National Hurricane Center, all of this information, as well
as radar data and reports from ships and ground observation, is
fed into giant computers. The meteorologists try to predict where
the storm is headed.

    This is a difficult job because changes in air pressure or air
currents can cause an abrupt shift in the storm's direction.

HURRICANE ANDREW
24 AUG 1992

926 MB

23

(left) Weather satellites help meteorologists track storms. This satellite picture shows Hurricane Andrew approaching the Florida coast. Andrew's path is traced from the time the storm first developed until it finally faded away on August 28.

(right) Andrew makes landfall in Miami-Dade County, Florida.

The hurricane can seem to be headed out to sea. Then it veers, and heads directly toward land.

Using all of the information they have gathered, the meteorologists at the National Hurricane Center predict that the storm the hurricane hunters have been following will make **landfall** in 48 hours—if it stays on its present course. And the hurricane hunters' latest data indicate that the winds have reached 100 mph.

The exhausted weather crew finally heads back to home base. Another plane will take their place in flying the dangerous *X* pattern through the hurricane. The wind speed is now up to 105 mph.

And the hurricane is less than 38 hours from land.

How a Hurricane Works

Tropical storms, including hurricanes, always form over warm ocean water, never inland. It is the warm ocean water that helps create the cycle that fuels a hurricane. Here's how it all works:

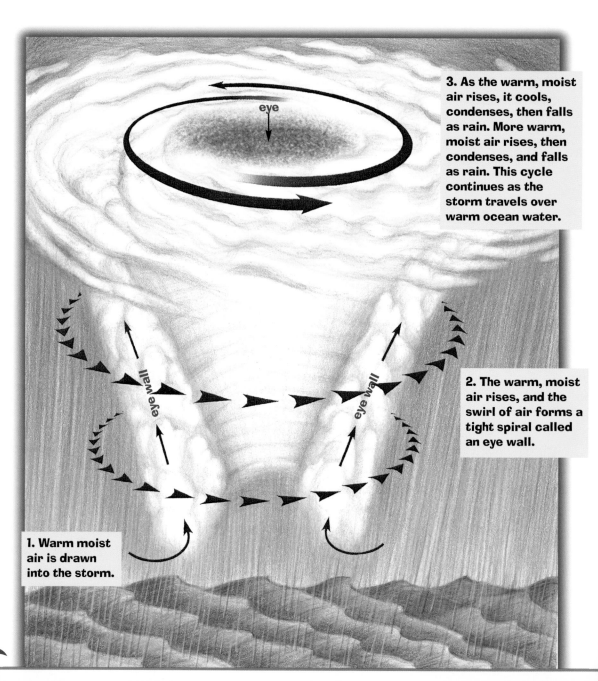

eye

eye wall

eye wall

3. As the warm, moist air rises, it cools, condenses, then falls as rain. More warm, moist air rises, then condenses, and falls as rain. This cycle continues as the storm travels over warm ocean water.

2. The warm, moist air rises, and the swirl of air forms a tight spiral called an eye wall.

1. Warm moist air is drawn into the storm.

Where Will It Strike?

The hurricane hunters report that the storm's winds are up to 115 mph. The meteorologists estimate that if the storm maintains its current speed and direction, it will hit land in 36 hours. The National Hurricane Center issues a **hurricane watch**.

People in the storm's path prepare a hurricane kit—filled with flashlights, batteries, drinking water, and other emergency supplies—if they don't already have one. Outdoor furniture and trash cans are taken inside so that they don't go flying when the wind starts. Cars are filled with gas, in case an evacuation is ordered. Windows are boarded up.

People stay close to radios and television. And they wait.

Meteorologists announce a hurricane watch when hurricane conditions may develop within 36 hours. A hurricane warning is issued when a hurricane is expected to hit land within 24 hours.

Workers must clear beaches of chairs, picnic tables, and any loose objects that can take flight when the wind starts to pick up.

The hurricane is now 26 hours from land. The next couple of hours are crucial for the weather scientists. They must decide whether people should evacuate the area in the hurricane's path.

Ordering an evacuation affects tens of thousands of people who live in the area. People must leave their homes and jobs. Businesses must close.

If the hurricane moves away from land after an evacuation is ordered, people will have suffered great hardships. And the next time an evacuation is ordered, people will be less likely to heed the warning and leave. However, because conditions change rapidly and forecasts are not perfect, people need to be prepared for the worst.

This hurricane now packs winds of 120 mph. Winds of this force can tear the roofs off houses. Trees can be uprooted and go crashing against homes. Power lines can snap and lash about like long, deadly whips. The storm surge can hurl huge walls of water ashore.

The hurricane hunters, satellites, and other high-tech equipment are available to help predict the path of the hurricane. But the time is almost here when meteorologists at the National Hurricane Center will have to make decisions that will affect thousands of lives.

The people now in the hurricane's path, and a little more than 24 hours from its fury, can only take the suggested precautions and listen to the weather reports.

And wait.

People living near the ocean must evacuate many hours before a hurricane hits. Coastal roads can start to flood two to four hours before the storm hits.

Residents must travel inland to stay safe during a severe hurricane. Dangling traffic lights are just one of the hazards during a hurricane.

When the hurricane is almost 24 hours from land, preparations are made to issue a **hurricane warning**. Then, new data indicates that the storm has suddenly altered its course. It may move away from land. The storm's movement is erratic. But a decision must be made on whether to issue a warning and order an evacuation.

As though finally making up its mind, the hurricane swerves back to its original path. Its winds roar at 125 mph. The storm is 24 hours from land. A hurricane warning is issued.

So, too, is the order to evacuate.

The Hurricane Makes Landfall

Thousands of cars move slowly along every highway and road leading inland. People living near the coast where the hurricane will hit have been ordered to leave the area. The hurricane is 12 hours from making landfall. Already the wind is increasing in speed, and rain is falling harder.

An hour passes. So does another, and still another. The coastal area seems a watery, windswept ghost town. Traffic lights swing in the wind and blink red and green, but there are no drivers to pay them any attention.

Hurricane Betsy sent waves crashing into the first floor of this Miami Beach hotel. Imagine what it might have looked like inside.

The front of the storm is approaching. The wind now roars. The rain isn't falling. It's blowing in massive sheets. Anything loose starts to bang about and get tossed around. Signs and tree limbs are whipped back and forth. Branches go flying and slam against buildings.

The wind speed is now up to 135 mph. More branches are torn loose and fly about. Trees are uprooted. As they topple, they tear down power lines.

The wind starts to work under parts of roofs. Loose shingles are pried free. Some roofs, weakened by the wind, are ripped completely off buildings.

The roar of the wind gets louder and louder. It sounds as if a hundred trains are thundering through town.

Windows that aren't covered are shattered by flying objects or splintered by the force of the wind. Houses and other buildings without boarded windows are invaded by both the wind and rain.

Along the coast, what looks like fog is headed for the shore. It's a 15-foot storm surge. This mountain of water picks up anything in its path—boats, trees, signs, an old truck,

Hurricane waves sweep across a beach. Even this house, built on stilts, isn't safe from the rising water.

and an abandoned car—and hurls it like a battering ram against buildings. The water will race up rivers and creeks. Along with the heavy rain, it will flood inland areas.

Residents who don't listen to evacuation orders risk being trapped as the storm grows stronger.

Then, eerily, in the midst of the extreme destruction, all grows calm and quiet. The hurricane's eye is passing. But the calm lasts only a short time. Soon the second half of the hurricane roars into the area and brings more devastation.

Finally, the wind decreases. The rain begins to slack. The worst is over.

As a final sign of its destructive power, the hurricane unleashes a dozen tornadoes. They twist erratically about the countryside with winds estimated to reach 150 mph. They cut another path of destruction as they zigzag across the land.

The tornadoes last only a few minutes, and then the countryside, like the coast, is peaceful in the midst of all the devastation.

Classifying Hurricanes

Meteorologists use the **Saffir-Simpson scale** to classify hurricanes and to estimate the damage caused by a storm. The scale ranks hurricanes from a category 1 to a category 5.

CATEGORY 1
Damage Level: **Minimal**
Wind Speed: 74 mph–95 mph
Storm Surge: 4 feet–5 feet

CATEGORY 2
Damage Level: **Moderate**
Wind Speed: 96 mph–110 mph
Storm Surge: 6 feet–8 feet

CATEGORY 3
Damage Level: **Extensive**
Wind Speed: 111 mph–130 mph
Storm Surge: 9 feet–12 feet

CATEGORY 4
Damage Level: **Extreme**
Wind Speed: 131 mph–155 mph
Storm Surge: 13 feet–18 feet

CATEGORY 5
Damage Level: **Catastrophic**
Wind Speed: 156+ mph
Storm Surge: 19+ feet

The Aftermath

The destruction that the hurricane leaves behind is staggering. Uprooted trees block streets. Buildings are battered. Some have lost their roofs. The ground is littered with shingles, pieces of wood, and other debris. Broken glass is everywhere. A sailboat is beached in the middle of some railroad tracks.

Many streets are flooded. Sand is everywhere. There is a serious danger of fire because of broken gas lines. Downed electrical wires dangle from leaning poles.

Swarms of snakes, some poisonous, have been driven from their natural habitats. They slither frantically about the streets among the fallen trees and the ruined buildings.

Here's a bird's-eye view of the destruction Hurricane Andrew left in its wake after tearing through southern Florida in 1992. A category 4 hurricane, like Andrew, has the power to flatten an entire neighborhood.

Hurricanes can cause severe flooding hundreds of miles from the coast.

The National Guard is one of the first groups on the scene. They clear streets and keep looters out of damaged areas. Repair crews from the gas and electric companies come next. But it can take a long time to restore service.

The Salvation Army and Red Cross provide shelter, blankets, and medicine for hurricane victims. The Federal Emergency Management Agency soon arrives to help the community recover from the disaster. Only when it is completely safe are people allowed to return to their homes. Then, the insurance companies move in to help people rebuild what they've lost.

In the future, scientists may be able to develop even better tools to help them predict and track these monster storms. But hurricanes will always remain one of the most powerful forces in nature.

Volunteers help out after a storm by packing food and other supplies to aid hurricane victims.

Tornadoes and Other Windstorms

During the most devastating hurricanes, the winds can reach speeds of more than 150 mph. But it's not just during a hurricane that winds become such a destructive force. Tornadoes, blizzards, and dust storms also show the power of wind.

Dust Storms

When a windstorm hits desertlike land, it can blow the dry or sandy soil into a dust storm. The dust can bury huge areas under a mound of sand. The winds of a dust storm can travel about 30 mph, but can gust up to 60 mph.

Tornadoes

The winds of a tornado spin around in a funnel shape at speeds as high as 300 mph. In the United States, tornadoes are most commonly sighted in the section of the country that stretches from Texas to Nebraska, an area often called Tornado Alley. But tornadoes can strike anywhere, and some are caused by hurricanes.

Blizzards

A blizzard combines winds of 35 mph or more and so much falling or blowing snow that visibility is near zero. Temperatures are usually below 20°F. Blizzards can close airports and paralyze entire cities. In a severe blizzard, the winds are more than 45 mph and the temperature is near or below 10°F.

Glossary

eye: the calm, circular area of low pressure at the center of a hurricane

eye wall: the inner circle of thunderstorms surrounding the eye of the hurricane where the highest winds are found

hurricane hunters: crews who fly through hurricanes and other tropical storms to record data such as wind speeds, air pressure, and exact location

hurricane warning: public notification by television, newspaper, radio, or the Internet that a hurricane is expected to hit shore within twenty-four hours

hurricane watch: public notification by television, newspaper, radio, or the Internet that hurricane conditions may be possible within the next thirty-six hours

landfall: the point where a tropical storm or hurricane first reaches or hits land

low pressure: decrease in air pressure that occurs when hot air rises. It often ushers in stormy weather.

meteorologists: scientists who study and forecast the weather

Saffir-Simpson scale: the categories scientists use to classify hurricanes

storm surge: the large dome or wall of water, created by the hurricane winds pushing water forward, that hits coastal areas when a hurricane makes landfall or approaches the coast

tropical depression: a group of storms rotating around an area of low pressure

tropical storm: a low-pressure system with winds of less intensity than those of a hurricane

weather satellite: an object sent up into space to track weather, including watching the formation and development of storms

Index

Websites

Take a cyberflight with real hurricane hunters and learn more about hurricanes and other disasters at these Websites:

www.hurricanehunters.com.
ww2010.atmos.uiuc.edu/(Gh)/guides/mtr/hurr/home.rxml
hurricanes.noaa.gov
www.fema.gov/kids/hurr.htm